# THE
# FREE GIFT
## OF LIFE

8 INTERACTIVE BIBLE STUDIES FOR
SMALL GROUPS AND INDIVIDUALS

# GORDON CHENG

*The Free Gift of Life*
Second edition
© Matthias Media 2009

First published 2005

Matthias Media
(St Matthias Press Ltd ACN 067 558 365)
PO Box 225
Kingsford NSW 2032
Australia
Telephone: (02) 9663 1478; international: +61-2-9663-1478
Facsimile: (02) 9663 3265; international: +61-2-9663-3265
Email: info@matthiasmedia.com.au
Internet: www.matthiasmedia.com.au

Matthias Media (USA)
Telephone: 724 964 8152; international: +1-724-964-8152
Facsimile: 724 964 8166; international: +1-724-964-8166
Email: sales@matthiasmedia.com
Internet: www.matthiasmedia.com

ISBN 978 1 921441 60 8

Cover design and typesetting by Lankshear Design Pty Ltd.

# » CONTENTS

## »HOW TO MAKE THE MOST OF THESE STUDIES

### 1. What is an Interactive Bible Study?

Interactive Bible Studies are a bit like a guided tour of a famous city. They take you through a particular part of the Bible, helping you to know where to start, pointing out things along the way, suggesting avenues for further exploration, and making sure that you know how to get home. Like any good tour, the real purpose is to allow you to go exploring for yourself—to dive in, have a good look around, and discover for yourself the riches that God's word has in store.

In other words, these studies aim to provide stimulation and input and point you in the right direction, while leaving you to do plenty of the exploration and discovery yourself.

We hope that these studies will stimulate lots of 'interaction'—interaction with the Bible, with the things we've written, with your own current thoughts and attitudes, with other people as you discuss them, and with God as you talk to him about it all.

## 2. The format

Each study contains five main components:

- short sections of text that introduce, inform, summarize and challenge
- a set of numbered study questions that help you examine the passage and think through its meaning
- sidebars that provide extra bits of background or optional extra study ideas, especially regarding other relevant parts of the Bible
- an 'Implications' section that helps you think about what this passage means for you and your life today
- suggestions for thanksgiving and prayer as you close.

## 3. How to use these studies on your own

- Before you begin, pray that God would open your eyes to what he is saying in the Bible, and give you the spiritual strength to do something about it.
- Work through the study, reading the text, answering the questions about the Bible passage, and exploring the sidebars as you have time.
- Resist the temptation to skip over the 'Implications' and 'Give thanks and pray' sections at the end. It is important that we not only hear and understand God's word, but respond to it. These closing sections help us do that.
- Take what opportunities you can to talk to others about what you've learnt.

## 4. How to use these studies in a small group

- Much of the above applies to group study as well. The studies are suitable for structured Bible study or cell groups, as well as for more informal pairs and triplets. Get together with a friend or friends and work through them at your own pace; use them as the basis for regular Bible study with your spouse. You don't need the formal structure of a 'group' to gain maximum benefit.

- For small groups, it is *very useful* if group members can work through the study themselves *before* the group meets. The group discussion can take place comfortably in an hour (depending on how sidetracked you get!) if all the members have done some work in advance.
- The role of the group leader is to direct the course of the discussion and to try to draw the threads together at the end. This will mean a little extra preparation—underlining the sections of text to emphasize and read out loud, working out which questions are worth concentrating on, and being sure of the main thrust of the study. Leaders will also probably want to work out approximately how long they'd like to spend on each part.
- If your group members usually don't work through the study in advance, it's extra important that the leader prepares which parts to concentrate on, and which parts to glide past more quickly. In particular, the leader will need to select which of the 'Implications' to focus on.
- We haven't included an 'answer guide' to the questions in the studies. This is a deliberate move. We want to give you a guided tour of the Bible, not a lecture. There is more than enough in the text we have written and the questions we have asked to point you in what we think is the right direction. The rest is up to you.

## 5. Bible translation

Previous studies in our Interactive Bible Study series have assumed that most readers would be using the New International Version of the Bible. However, since the release of the English Standard Version in 2001, many have switched to the ESV for study purposes. For this reason, we have decided to quote from and refer to the ESV text, which we recommend.

# THE GOSPEL ACCORDING TO PAUL

## [ROMANS 1:1-17]

DESPITE THE NUMBER OF commentaries on the book of Romans, it is not a hard letter to understand. That is to say, it is no harder than the gospel it contains, which is at one and the same time so simple that a child may be saved by it, yet containing all sorts of traps for those who don't want to hear what God says to them. The amount written over the centuries on the book of Romans could be taken as an indication of how difficult it is to unlock Paul's meaning, and it is certainly true that there is a lot to be gained from studying Romans carefully and thoughtfully. But the books that have been written about Romans are better understood as an outpouring of gratitude for the kindness God has shown in so clearly teaching the message of the gospel through his servant Paul. Those who trust Jesus should approach this letter with a similar confidence to the original Roman recipients: the confidence that there is great blessing to be gained in what Paul, and Paul's Lord, desire to impart to us.

1. By looking at the following passages, what clues can you discover about Paul and why he is writing to the Christians in Rome? What is occupying his mind?

   • Romans 1:1-17

   • Romans 9:1-6

   • Romans 15:14-33

## Tricky words

**v. 1—'Apostle':** Paul says that he was called to be "an apostle". We know from Acts 1:21-26 that an apostle is someone who was with Jesus in his earthly ministry and was a witness of his resurrection. Given the highly unusual circumstances of his becoming a witness to the resurrection, it's not surprising that Paul would refer to himself as "one untimely born" and as the "least of the apostles" (1 Cor 15:8-9). Acts 9:1-16 gives a spectacular account of Paul's commissioning ▶

2. What do we learn about Paul himself from the following verses?

   • Romans 1:1

   • Romans 15:14-33

**3.** In Romans 1:1-4, Paul moves straight from his greeting to the heart of the gospel.

- Who is the gospel about?

- What do you learn about the person whom the gospel is about?

**4.** According to Romans 1:5:

- What is the right response to the gospel?

- Who is the gospel for?

as an apostle. Here we see just how unusual his coming to Christ was, and—very importantly—we learn that he will have a particular concern to bring the gospel news to the non-Jews (the 'Gentiles').

**v. 1—'Servant of the Lord':** this is a very humble title (the Greek word used here for 'servant' is the normal word for 'slave') but it also carries some weight of authority with it as well. The 'Servant of the Lord' is a figure whose mission of rescue of God's people is prophesied in the second half of the book of Isaiah, and fulfilled by Jesus in his life, death and resurrection. Paul sees himself as fulfilling this same mission! (See Acts 13:47, citing Isaiah 49 concerning the Servant.) Even though the title is humble, then, it is also a claim that his mission is to be taken seriously, because it is an extension of the mission of Jesus.

**v. 4—'Son of God':** At first glance, this looks like a claim that Jesus is God, as in 'God, the Son'. While it is true that Jesus *is* God and that Paul believed it, it is not at the heart of what he means here. In the Old Testament, the Davidic King of Israel was from time to time referred to as God's own 'son', who would rule forever over God's kingdom (see 2 Sam 7:12-14; Ps 2:7; Ps 89:20-26). What Paul ▶

is saying here is that Jesus, descended from David, is the kingly 'son of God', who fulfils all the marvellous promises made by God about the Messiah. This also helps us understand how Jesus is *declared* to be the Son of God by his resurrection: he has always been God's Son from eternity; but now, in his mighty resurrection, his authority as God's appointed Messiah and Lord—the 'Son of God'—has been sealed (cf. Acts 2:36).

**v. 17—'from faith for faith':** This slightly puzzling phrase could have a number of possible meanings. It could mean that an act of faithfulness on the part of God— the sending of Jesus to die on the cross—has the result or intention of producing faith in us. It could mean that Christian faith begins with the Old Testament faith and moves to the faith that we place in Jesus. A number of other options have been suggested, but what is clearly excluded is any idea that being right with God is dependent upon human action. The option that might best reflect this is to reword the literal phrase "from faith to faith" as something describing a righteousness that is 'completely by faith, with no other contribution from any good thing that we might imagine we have to offer'.

## Read Romans 1:8–17.

**5.** Why does Paul want to visit Rome? What is specific to him as an apostle, and what can we copy from his example?

**6.** Look carefully at how the repeated word 'for' links together the ideas in verses 15, 16 and 17.

- Why is Paul eager to preach in Rome?

- Why is he not ashamed of the gospel?

- Why is the gospel the power of God for salvation?

# What's this letter about?

IN ROMANS 1 WE MEET a massive racial divide—between those who are Jews, the sons of Abraham and the heirs of all God's Old Testament promises, and those who are not. The name given to non-Jews is 'Gentiles', sometimes translated (for example in 1:5) as "the nations". In this way, we are led into a number of major themes in the letter. These themes include:

- how knowledge of God is possible (through the gospel of Jesus)
- where God's promises to the Jews fit in (he keeps them, in Jesus)
- how the Gentiles will get right with God (the same way as the Jews: through Jesus)
- how the Gentiles will hear the gospel of Jesus (through God's apostle, Paul, with the financial help of the Romans, and ultimately through a mission that all who trust Jesus are a part of)
- how Jews and Gentiles should now live together
- and perhaps the most significant theme of all: how can God declare that unrighteous people (both Jews and Gentiles) are *not* unrighteous but righteous, yet still remain true to his own righteous character?

The last of these themes—'righteousness'—is an extremely important concept in Romans, and it appears for the first time in Romans in the famous **verses 16-17**:

> For I am not ashamed of the gospel, for it is the power of God for salvation to everyone who believes, to the Jew first and also to the Greek. For in it the righteousness of God is revealed from faith for faith, as it is written, "The righteous shall live by faith".

What does 'righteousness' mean? We tend to think of a 'righteous' person as someone who is extremely moral or upright in character. This is true as far as it goes, but in the Bible, righteousness is essentially about being declared to be moral and 'in the right' before the judge. To be righteous is to be declared 'not guilty' in court; to

## Verse 17

The other curious thing about verse 17 is its quotation of Habakkuk 2:4: "The righteous shall live by his faith".

Habakkuk is a short Old Testament book almost certainly written about how God calls up the ancient and wicked empire of Babylon to punish his own people. At first, it appears to Habakkuk as a cruel and unusual punishment—like hiring a Mafia hit man to instil family discipline.

By the end of the book, however, Habakkuk has been satisfied by the assurance God gives that this is not vindictive retribution against Israel. All unrighteousness everywhere—Israel's, Babylon's, and that of all other people and nations —will be judged by a God who is personally angered and offended by human rebellion. Habakkuk may witness some of this destruction in his own lifetime but he, and all like him, will continue to trust that God will bring salvation out of the darkest sin and wickedness.

So the book of Habakkuk ends with Habakkuk rejoicing and continuing to look to God for his salvation, despite the sin, wickedness and divine judgement that surrounds him.

be pronounced innocent and blameless before the law. It's to be publicly vindicated as having done what is right and lawful.

In normal circumstances, people are declared 'not guilty' because in fact they are not guilty. God himself, for example, is perfectly righteous, because he is always in the right, keeping every single promise, and always acting in accordance with his perfectly good character. However, we are not righteous—quite the opposite. Were we to stand before God as our judge and give account for our behaviour towards him and towards others, we would be anything but blameless and 'not guilty'.

How then can we ever be declared righteous by God? How can we ever stand before him without being condemned?

The key that helps us to unlock Romans is seeing that the *only* righteousness it is possible for humans to have is the righteousness that comes as a free gift, through Jesus Christ. It can never be a righteousness that comes through our own hard work in living up to the standard of God's glory and perfect holiness. Once this is understood, the other blessings of Paul's letter unfold to our great comfort and joy, and to the glory of God.

## » Implications

(Choose one or more of the following to think about further or to discuss in your group.)

* Why do you think Paul quotes Habakkuk 2:4 in Romans 1:17? What point do you think he's making?

- Think back over what you have learnt about the nature of the gospel and how we should respond to it. What challenges does this understanding bring to:

  - your own life?

  - your small group?

  - your church?

- What reasons can you find in Romans 1:1-17 for being involved in spreading the gospel to others?

- According to Romans 1:1-17, how are we saved? How should this view of salvation affect:

  - our view of ourselves?

  - our view of others?

## » Give thanks and pray

- Give thanks for the riches to be found in the book of Romans, and pray that the Holy Spirit would help you to hear God's voice in the coming weeks.
- Give thanks for the gospel: "the power of God for salvation to everyone who believes".
- What else does this passage prompt you to give thanks and to pray for?

# GOD'S ANGER, HUMANITY'S SIN

## [ROMANS 1:18-32]

D OES GOD GET ANGRY? CHRISTIANS and non-Christians alike are universally delighted to affirm that "God is love". But there is some anxiety, even hostility, to the suggestion that God might be angry with us.

The trouble is, Romans 1 goes on to say that not only does God get angry, but that his anger is on display here and now.

**Read Romans 1:17-20.**

**1.** Look at verses 17 and 18. What similarities do you notice between them?

**2.** How is God's righteousness revealed to those without faith?

**3.** What exactly can be known about God from creation? Compare Psalm 19:1-6. How do we naturally respond to this knowledge?

**4.** According to Romans 1:18-20, why is it fair that God's wrath should be revealed?

# The wrath of God

THOSE WHO WANT TO TREAT THE Bible seriously will rightly point out that love and anger are not incompatible, either in humans or in God. Rather, it is *indifference* that really demonstrates a lack of love. God's anger is clearly part of his character, and is often referred to in the Scriptures.

Some respond to this by suggesting that whenever the Bible speaks of God's wrath, it is really speaking not of actual anger, but of the natural, impersonal consequences of our own sin, which God allows us to suffer because he respects our choices.

To speak of the *natural* consequences of sin is at one level completely true. The man who aims and shoots the gun should not be surprised if the person he aims at is hurt, nor should he be surprized when the favour is returned. To view the suffering that sin causes as a logical (if unpleasant) result makes good sense of the world in which we live in, and of our own experience of it.

But when we look at sin and its consequences as Christians, we need to begin not with our observation of the world, but with what the Bible teaches that God is doing in his creation. It's only in the light of what God says in Scripture that we can begin to make sense of the world and the sin and suffering we see.

When we look at the evidence of this passage, we discover the uncomfortable truth that God is personally offended by our sins. It is the same discovery that Habakkuk had been reminded of so many years earlier. Uncomfortable as this discovery is, it is only through becoming aware of God's personal anger against those who sin that the incredible depth of his personal love for us will become clear.

## Read Romans 1:18-32.

5. Fill in the following table. If you are in a small group, compare answers and observations.

| Passage | Actions described | Consequences |
|---|---|---|
| 1:18-25 | | |
| 1:26-27 | | |

| Passage | Actions described | Consequences |
|---------|-------------------|--------------|
| 1:28–32 |                   |              |

**6.** What action is God spoken of as performing three times (1:24, 26, 28)?

**7.** What can you conclude, therefore, about:

- the nature of sin?

- the nature of judgement?

**8.** Look up these verses and summarize either the criticisms made, or the expectations set out (note also who is being addressed):

- Leviticus 18:22

- Deuteronomy 4:16-18

- 2 Kings 17:15

- Psalm 106:20

- Isaiah 44:19-20

- Jeremiah 2:5

- Jeremiah 10:14

**9.** Comparing the list with Romans 1:18-32, what similarities can you see? Is the sinfulness described by Paul just a Gentile problem? Why/why not?

## » Implications

(Choose one or more of the following to think about further or to discuss in your group.)

- Do people know God without having heard the gospel? Why or why not?

- What is it that lies at the heart of sin?

- How do you react to the idea of God's anger being revealed *now* against wickedness? Does it offend you? Can you think of examples in your own life?

- From what you have learned in Romans 1:18-23, how would you respond to these statements?

  - "I believe all religions have something of the truth."

  - "I believe all religions are an attempt to seek God."

  - "I believe very few people could be described as truly evil."

  - "If homosexuality is genetic, then it's not a sin."

  - "It's discouraging and off-putting for Christians to talk so much about sin and judgement."

- "Perhaps the God of the Old Testament was an angry God, but the religion of Jesus is about love, tolerance and embracing everyone without distinction."

- Can you think of examples of how people claim to be wise, yet become fools (1:22)?

- What difference will it make to us to understand that Romans 1:18-32 is also true of our friends and family?

## » Give thanks and pray

- Thank God for his character: the way that he displays both great love and true righteousness to us now.
- Thank God for providing the payment for our sin and rebellion in his Son, Jesus Christ.
- Ask God to give us the humility to listen to the message of sin and judgement in Romans, and to change the things we need to change.

# GIVE ME JUSTICE!

## [ROMANS 2]

IT IS A DEMAND THAT CAN BE FOUND IN every culture or society, in any period of history: "Give me justice!" But what does it mean? And if we knew, would we really want it? Romans works from the position that only God is just, and that only God can give true justice to those who want it (and to those who don't). It's crucial that this be the case, otherwise Paul's entire case that we deserve to be judged by God falls apart. There is a great deal at stake, because all of humanity is being called to account.

---

**Read Romans 2:1–11.**

**1.** Describe the person condemned in verse 1. How might they respond to the sins described in Romans 1:18-32? What is Paul's message to them?

---

**2.** What do we learn about the character of God from the way he treats us?

**3.** When will God's patience run out?

**4.** According to Romans 2:1-11:

- on what basis is someone *judged* on the day of wrath?

- on what basis is someone *saved* from the day of wrath?

**5.** Following on from question 4, will there be anyone who fulfils the criteria of verses 7 and 10, and who will therefore receive a good reward on the day of wrath? (Recall any relevant discussion from study 2.)

**NB.** For some detailed comments on verses 6-10, and the possibility that some people might earn eternal life by 'doing good', see the appendix on page 69.

# Was Israel's failure God's failure?

THE LAW PROVED TO BE A MIXED blessing to the Jews, as Paul points out here in Romans in his outlining of "my gospel" (2:16). Of course, all Jews were familiar with the promise of either life or death that **the law** contained (Deut 30:15-20), a promise that was not directly available to the Gentiles unless they decided to convert to Judaism. This placed the Jews in a position of enormous privilege and responsibility. They had the privilege of having God's life-giving law; they had the responsibility of following it perfectly and, in so doing, showing God's glory to the nations outside. The intention was that non-Jews would see God's glory and come to know him through the living witness of his people.

When the Jews failed to obey, the curses of the law spelt out in Deuteronomy 28-30 came to pass. The law had failed to bring life, because the nation Israel had failed to respond as it ought. Finally, Jesus' death on the cross, as the ultimate sacrifice to take away the guilt of sin, brought the temple sacrificial system to an end (Mark 15:38). The Jewish sacrificial system for dealing with sin had been fulfilled and so ended in Christ's death.

Did this mean an end to Jewish privilege? Even more importantly, did it mean that God had in some way failed? He had promised to bless the children of Abraham (Gen 12:1-3). He had given them the indescribable privilege of being the bearers of his word, the law, so that they might have the life he promised to give them (see Psalm 119 for a classic statement of how wonderful God's law was). Yet they had neither kept that law nor, in consequence, received the blessing. On the contrary—on account of his righteousness, God had cursed them.

What then of God's promises to rescue and save Israel? Could a God who failed to keep a promise, even for reasons of his righteousness, truly be said to be righteous? Surely better could be expected of a promise-keeping God?

The righteous character of God is an issue of fundamental importance, not only for the Jewish people but for anyone who entrusts themselves to God's justice and mercy.

## What is 'the law'?

The word 'law' in the Bible can mean a number of things. Usually, when it's not meaning the whole of the Old Testament (or sometimes, the first five books), it means the 'law' given through Moses to Israel at Mt Sinai, especially the Ten Commandments (Exod 20:1-17). These Ten Commandments, in turn, are usually linked with all the Old Testament laws (together with specific examples) that gave instruction to God's people living in the land of Israel before the coming of Jesus. Some Christians find it useful to divide these various laws into three categories: moral, ceremonial and civic. This is helpful, as long as it's recognized that the Bible itself doesn't divide the law in this way. Rather, the Bible insists that while some matters of the law are weightier than others, the law must nonetheless be viewed as one and obeyed in its entirety. As James 2:10 says, "For whoever keeps the whole law but fails in one point has become accountable for all of it" (cf. Gal 3:10; Deut 27:26).

In Romans, we see that Paul, the Jewish ex-rabbi, now preached Jesus. But he saw himself not as moving away from the law, but rather as demonstrating that the entire law, indeed all of God's Old Testament promises to the Jews, were fulfilled in Christ.

**Read Romans 2:12–16.**

**6.** What law is being referred to? (Note v. 14.)

**7.** How could someone, in theory, be justified (declared 'not guilty') by the law?

**8.** Are any Gentiles "doers of the law"? Is anyone a "doer of the law"?

**Read Romans 2:17–29.**

**9.** How would you summarize the problem of the person described in verses 17-24?

**10.** Who is a true Jew?

**11.** According to Paul's argument so far, do you think there are any true Jews?

## Some cutting observations

BY THIS STAGE OF THE ARGUMENT, Paul has radically undercut some of the pomposity of those who see themselves as superior to the degenerate sinners of chapter 1. He has reminded his readers that God is perfectly just and fair, and that everyone will be exposed as sinful by his perfect standard of righteousness. But the Jewish sense of privilege rested on more than simply moral behaviour, however far they fell short of the required standard in reality.

The Jews knew that they were privileged simply because they had the law, and so could take pride in being those especially chosen and marked out by their physical circumcision—the cutting away of the male foreskin—and their other legal distinctions such as food laws, ritual cleanliness and temple worship. But as Paul points out, not even these privileges help the Jews to gain right standing with God, because true Jewishness was never, and will never be, a matter of mere outward observance. It is a matter of inward heart-obedience, wrought by the Spirit of God.

## » Implications

(Choose one or more of the following to think about further or to discuss in your group.)

- Judging by Paul's teaching from Romans 1:18 to the end of chapter 2, are there any grounds for hoping that we might be saved from God's wrath? Why/Why not?

- Why is it important to be clear about how sinful humans are:

  - with respect to understanding what we can do about it?

  - with respect to the rightness of God's judgement?

- What does this chapter teach us about how to please God?

## » Give thanks and pray

- Thank God for being incredibly faithful to his promises to his people, even to a people that is not faithful to him.
- Pray that, through Christ, we will be people of inward righteousness, not just outward appearance.

# LAW WITHOUT LOOPHOLES

## [ROMANS 3:1-20]

THE GRIM VERDICT ABOUT the *unrighteousness* of all humanity in **chapters 1 and 2** leads to a further, deeper question about righteousness—and that is God's righteousness. Is it fair of God to condemn the Jews? After all, they had been promised the blessing of God, and had received it in the form of the law of God. If God now condemns them, significant doubt might be thrown on whether he really is acting justly.

Paul vigorously denies any injustice on God's part. But it is a measure of how serious this objection is, and how difficult it is to overcome, that it will not be fully answered until the end of Romans 11. Here, Paul begins to address at least some of the objections that a Jew might have to his argument so far.

**The story so far**

To summarize where we've come to:

- In 1:16-17, Paul introduces what will be the major theme of his letter: the righteousness of God. In the rest of chapter 1, he shows how God, in his righteousness, is angry with all the "ungodliness and unrighteousness of men".
- In chapter 2, he cuts the ground away from any Jewish objectors who might consider themselves to be more 'righteous' than the godless people talked about in chapter 1. God's righteous judgement will come upon them too, because having the law is no advantage if you don't keep it—and they don't.

**Read Romans 3:1–8.**

**1.** Why might a Jew imagine that he had an advantage over the non-Jew?

**2.** According to these verses, does Paul agree or disagree? On what grounds?

**3.** Imagine you were compiling evidence for a debate on the following topic: "Is it right of God to condemn the Jews?" Jot the evidence down in two columns:

| God's fairness: the case for | God's fairness: the case against |
| --- | --- |
| | |

*Group activity:* If you're in a small group, you might like to split the group in two, and set up an actual debate on the topic with the group leader as adjudicator. Spend 10 minutes going through the passage in separate groups, and then give one or two speakers from each group two minutes each to argue the case. Team A argues that God is being unfair in the way he treats the Jews. Team B argues that God is being perfectly fair. At the end of the debate the group leader sums up and adjudicates.

4. "Why not do evil that good may come?" (v. 8). What is there in what Paul has said that might lead people to claim this?

5. Read Psalm 51:1-5 in context. How is God "justified" (vindicated or declared right) by declaring people guilty?

**Read Romans 3:9-20.**

**6.** Paul quotes these verses listed below. Look them up and summarize what they are saying in their original context. (If you're working in a small group, divide the verses among the group.)

- Psalm 14:1-3

- Psalm 53:1-3

- Psalm 5:9

- Psalm 140:3

- Psalm 10:7

- Proverbs 1:16

- Isaiah 59:7-8

- Psalm 36:1

**7.** Why do you think Paul quotes all these verses, rather than (for example) simply saying what he thinks in his own words?

**8.** What major conclusion does this passage reach?

# Failing the test

THE JEW HAS AN ENORMOUS AMOUNT to be proud of. Yet by the time we have considered both the causes for pride, and the reasons why these are not worth a great deal in gaining right standing with God, we realize that the whole of humanity is in a terrible predicament of its own doing.

It's as if the whole world were due to sit an exam.

Some—the Jews—have been privileged to be enrolled in a special series of personal lectures by the Examiner that covers the exam material in great detail, and makes stunningly clear exactly what is required to pass. The rest—the Gentiles —have had no direct contact with the Examiner whatsoever, but they nevertheless have been supplied with all the information they need in order to pass.

Both groups have all they need to pass the exam with flying colours. Both have plenty of time to prepare. But in the end, when the exam is finally held, it is discovered that every single person has failed. Not one of the students has been attentive and wise enough to take in what they were learning and apply it. And now all will face the consequences.

Were the Jews privileged to have been granted such special access? Certainly. But in the end, it did them no good, for they failed the test just as badly as the rest. And can the Gentiles complain? Not at all, because God wrote his study notes in big letters all over his creation, but they ignored and suppressed that knowledge, and turned to idolatry and wickedness instead (1:18ff). God is quite justified in writing a large red F on everybody's paper, "so that every mouth may be stopped, and the whole world may be held accountable to God" (3:19).

## » Implications

(Choose one or more of the following to think about further or to discuss in your group.)

- Using this passage and the rest of Romans to this point, how would you define 'sin'?

- How do you think sin is expressed in:

  - thoughts?

  - attitudes?

- actions?

- relationship with others?

- relationship with God?

- "I can't believe that everybody is as bad as Paul says we are." What do you think? How does Paul make his point?

- How would you use the arguments of Romans 1:18-3:20 to convince a friend who behaved well (and knew it) that they were sinful?

## » Give thanks and pray

- Thank God for being true, though every man is a liar (3:4).
- Pray for change and forgiveness if this passage has confronted you about any particular sin in your life.

# THE HEART OF THE GOSPEL

## [ROMANS 3:21-26]

The chief point, and the very central place of the Epistle, and of the whole Bible.

THAT'S HOW MARTIN LUTHER, THE famous 16th-century Reformer, described the six verses of Romans 3:21-26. There is no question that what Paul says here is utterly basic to the teaching of the Bible: the message that we can't be right with God through our own good works or religiosity, but only by trusting in the death of Jesus on our behalf.

While it would be unwise to expect these few verses to explain everything that Jesus achieved on the cross on our behalf, nevertheless the ideas explained here are so crucial—in every sense—that if we misunderstand this passage, we misunderstand not only the whole of Romans but also the meaning of the cross itself. This is why we are devoting an entire study to such a short section.

One helpful indication as to the importance and meaning of these verses is that the expression "the righteousness of God" pops up again in 3:21. We've already discussed, back in study 1, just how important the idea of 'righteousness' is. By picking up the term here, Paul reminds us of an idea that is absolutely basic to Romans: how God's righteousness is known and laid hold of by sinful people. From 1:18-3:20 various tempting possibilities for gaining righteousness (or possibly avoiding its demands!) have been considered and firmly shut down.

Now, for the first time since the beginning of the letter, Paul returns to consider the work of Christ on the cross.

1. From Romans 1:18-3:20, Paul has been arguing one key idea about what people are like. What is it? Are you convinced? Spend a few moments reviewing and summarizing what has been said.

**Read Romans 3:21-26.**

(Because this is such an important passage, and so closely argued, we've included a translation of it here so that all group members can be working from the same text. It's the text of the English Standard Version, slightly modified in verse 22.)

[21]But now the righteousness of God has been manifested apart from the law, although the Law and the Prophets bear witness to it—[22]the righteousness of God through the faithfulness[1] of Jesus Christ for all who believe. For there is no distinction: [23]for all have sinned and fall short of the glory of God, [24]and are justified by his grace as a gift, through the redemption that is in Christ Jesus, [25]whom God put forward as a propitiation by his blood, to be received by faith. This was to show God's righteousness, because in his divine forbearance he had passed over former sins. [26]It was to show his righteousness at the present time, so that he might be just and the justifier of the one who has faith in Jesus.

2. The word "But" in verse 21 means that Paul is now moving on to make a new point. What is that point?

**3.** What is the role of the law:

- according to verse 19?

- according to verse 21?

**4.** How did Jesus show "faithfulness" (3:22)? How does his faithfulness contrast with humanity's (in 1:18-3:20 and 3:23)?

**5.** On what basis can Paul say in 3:23 that "all have sinned and fall short of the glory of God"?

**6.** According to 3:24-25:

**a.** What happens by grace?

**b.** Exactly how are we "justified", that is, made right with God?

## Redemption and propitiation

In this passage there are a number of important words that are used by the Bible and by Christians, but not always understood. The words "righteousness", "justification" and "law" have already been mentioned; two other words should now be particularly noted: *redemption* and *propitiation*.

'Redemption' has its roots in the experience of Israel in Egypt under Pharaoh, before they were led out by Moses from their slavery. The story is found in Exodus, and is referred to again and again in the course of Israel's subsequent history. It is a defining moment for the nation, like the War of Independence in the USA, the signing of the Magna Carta in ▶

**c.** What does the word **'redemption'** suggest about our life before we became Christians, and our life after?

**d.** What does the word **'propitiation'** suggest about our life before we became Christians, and our life after?

**e.** What does "by his blood" mean in verse 25?

**f.** What do these two verses say about what it means to become a Christian?

**7.** According to Paul's argument in these verses, how does the cross manage to demonstrate *both* God's mercy *and* his justice?

Britain, or the Anzac legend of courage under fire for Australians and New Zealanders.

Essentially, redemption is the payment of a price to release someone or something from a form of bondage—such as slavery or some economic captivity—after which the thing redeemed belongs to the one who paid the price. Israel was 'redeemed' from the judgement that Egypt fell under when every firstborn male in the land died at the hand of God's angel of death. The Israelites were spared, because they had redeemed the lives of their firstborn sons by the sacrifice of the Passover lamb. Once the blood of the Passover lamb was placed on the door of the house, the angel of death 'passed over' the firstborn of Israel, and so Israel was said to have been redeemed from the judgement of God. This redemption by the death of a sacrifice signalled their ownership by God, and their release and rescue from slavery to Egypt.

Our understanding of **'propitiation'** likewise is grounded in the experience of Israel. Propitiation literally means the averting of anger (in this case, God's) by the offering of a sacrifice. The entire Old Testament sacrificial system had at its heart the death of bulls, goats and sheep to pay the penalty for sin (as Romans 6:23 says, "the wages of sin is death"). By offering the blood of the sacrifice instead of the blood of the guilty ▶

person, God was 'propitiated'—that is, his anger was turned aside.

Some Christians, disturbed at the thought that God might be angry, attempt to tone down the word 'propitiation' in Romans 3:25 in various ways. Some argue, for example, that God's justice or judgement is impersonal —that he is not actually angry with sin, but merely that sin has natural consequences, and that these natural consequences can be referred to as 'God's judgement'. Some translations (such as the RSV) accordingly translated the word in verse 25 as 'expiation', which means not the averting of God's anger, but the less offensive idea of the wiping away of sin (along with its natural consequences). 'Expiation' operates on the sinner— his sin is blotted out. 'Propitiation' operates on God—it turns aside his righteous wrath against sinners.

In the end, only 'propitiation' does justice to the meaning of the word in Romans 3:25, its immediate context, and the argument of Romans to this point. Our sin is not to be understood as an impersonal act with certain natural consequences. At its heart, sin is a personal rejection of God and his kingly authority. And God's response to it is also personal. He is rightly angry, and his anger is put aside only in the propitiatory death of his Son.

## » Implications

(Choose one or more of the following to think about further or to discuss in your group.)

- A friend says, "Anyone who is sure they are going to heaven is arrogant and presumptuous". How could you use verse 24 to answer this objection?

- How could you use any of these ideas about Jesus' death to comfort someone who feels guilty or ashamed about their sin?

- How does the cross benefit God—that is, what's in it for him?

- Some modern theologians describe the idea of God punishing his son as a form of 'divine child abuse'. How could you answer this objection from the passage?

- "We can't ever understand the cross, so we shouldn't try. The Christian faith is too intellectual anyway." How would you respond to this?

- How does the death of Jesus in Romans 3:21-26 affect:
  - our sense of worth?

  - the cause of our guilt?

  - our certainty about the future?

  - our anxiety about God's anger and judgement?

  - our need to impress God or others?

## » Give thanks and pray

- Thank God for his gift of redemption in Christ Jesus, that we can accept by faith.
- Thank God for Jesus, that though he was sinless, yet he bore the penalty for our rebellion and rejection of God.
- Pray that we might continue to understand more fully how God alone is the one who is just and the justifier of the one who has faith in Jesus.

**Endnote**

1. Nearly all modern translations render this phrase as 'faith in Jesus Christ'. However, there are very good reasons for translating it as 'the faith (or faithfulness) of Jesus Christ'.

# FAITH ALONE

## [ROMANS 3:27-4:25]

1. Think back over the first few chapters of Romans that we have studied, and then read Romans 3:27-31. How might you feel about Paul's argument so far:

   • if you were a Jew?

   • if you were a Gentile?

# Father Abraham had many sons

FOR JEWS, PAUL'S MESSAGE WAS revolutionary—as it was for Paul himself, when he first realized its truth on the road to Damascus. That message? That the law of Moses could not bring justification; the only thing that could put us right with God was faith in the risen Lord Jesus Christ. The law, in which pious Jews had placed so much hope, was not going to be of any use at all in initiating or fostering relationship with God, except in pointing out the need for God's grace and forgiveness.

Perhaps even more shocking was the incredible implication of faith in Jesus Christ. If justification was available to *everyone* who believes, then it was available to Gentiles as well as Jews—on the same basis!

For the Jew, all this was hard to take. If justification was *apart from the law*, where does that leave the law? Is Paul saying that the law is rubbish? Was the entire Old Testament just a waste of time, now to be swept away by this new teaching? It sounds as if Paul is being an absolute traitor to his Jewish identity and ancestry.

"On the contrary", says Paul. "I'm not overthrowing the law, I'm upholding it". And to prove the point, he opens up the law (that is, the Torah, the first five books of the Old Testament), and speaks about the forefather of all the Jews: Abraham.

## Context

In Genesis 12:1-3, Abraham was promised the blessing of God. The blessing was stated unconditionally: a land to live in, many descendants, and God blessing those who blessed Abraham (and his descendants) and cursing those who cursed Abraham (and his descendants). In Genesis 15, God visits Abraham and repeats his intention to bless him.

## Read Genesis 15:1-6.

2. What promises does Abraham receive? How does he respond?

**Read Romans 4:1-5.**

**3.** How does Abraham's example back up Paul's argument?

**4.** How does Paul explain the word "counted" (or 'reckoned')?

**5.** Romans 4:5 describes God as the one who "justifies the ungodly". What is the moral problem here? (Compare God's character as described in Genesis 18:25.)

**6.** How has Paul dealt with the moral problem of Romans 4:5 in Romans 1-3? How does he deal with it in Abraham's case?

## David's sin

If Abraham was the father of all true Jews, from before Moses came and passed on God's law, then the next great hero of Israel's faith was King David, who came to the throne when the demands and promises of the law were clear and explicit. But David went from hero to zero when he committed adultery with Bathsheba and then engineered the murder of her husband Uriah.

## Read Romans 4:6–25.

**7.** Paul now quotes one of **David's** psalms, where he talks about his sinfulness and God's forgiveness (Psalm 32). How does the example of David, and the quote from Psalm 32 in verses 7-8, back up Paul's message about how we get right with God?

**8.** David received this blessing of forgiveness as a circumcised Jew under the Mosaic Law. But is it only available to the circumcised? How does Paul answer this in verses 9-12?

**9.** According to verses 13-15, how does keeping the law wipe out the effectiveness of faith?

**10.** How does faith make the promise effective, according to verse 16?

**11.** In verses 23-25, what things that God has done and promised should we be placing our trust in? What will happen when we do?

# Faith means what?

'FAITH' AND 'BELIEF' ARE THE SAME thing in the Bible (in fact, there is only one Greek word, and we use the two different English words mainly for stylistic reasons). The idea of faith or belief includes the idea of reliance or trust in the object of faith, not simply intellectual assent. If I trust the pilot of the plane, it means I will step on board and follow his instructions. If I say I trust him but refuse to enter the aircraft, it is quite fair to assume that I don't really trust him.

In Genesis, although God's promise to Abraham is completely unconditional, it's necessary for Abraham to respond by believing that God will indeed give him a land, blessing and descendants. This last promise seemed highly unlikely, given Abraham's age and that of his wife, Sarah. Both were long past the age where they might reasonably expect to bear children by normal means. At a number of points, however, it becomes clear that Abraham trusts God implicitly—hence the quoting of

Genesis 15:6 in Romans 4:3: "Abraham believed God, and it was counted to him as righteousness". Abraham knew that God would not fail to keep his promises, and so at length a son, Isaac, was born to Abraham and Sarah. It was Abraham's trust, not his works, that brought him into perfect, right relationship with his God. God, then, is the one who brought this righteousness about.

The most vivid example of this faith is found in Genesis 22. Abraham realized that even if his only son, Isaac, heir of God's promise, should be killed in a sacrifice, God would still keep his promise on the other side of death. Abraham's faith didn't waver at any stage. So Abraham is held up as the example of what true faith looks like. We need to consider, then, what it means to follow that example.

## » Implications

(Choose one or more of the following to think about further or to discuss in your group.)

• Romans 4:16 says that Abraham is "the father of us all". What does this mean, and how should we apply it to ourselves?

• Note down briefly how God is at work in this chapter:

  • in Abraham

  • in David

- in us

- in Jesus

- Following on from this, what would you say you have learned about:
  - God's character?

  - God's power?

- In what ways do you feel you are sometimes tempted to try to earn God's approval by your own good works? What things do you do that you are quietly proud of before God?

## » Give thanks and pray

- Give thanks for the faith of Abraham, and that we can be his spiritual offspring, having our faith counted to us as righteousness.
- Pray that we will know that God is able to do as he has promised.

# SOMETHING TO BOAST ABOUT

## [ROMANS 5:1-11]

W HEN WE REACH ROMANS 5, we reach another key stage in Paul's argument. The climax of the argument so far occurred in 3:21-26, where Paul unveiled how we are justified only through trusting in Jesus' faithful work. Now, in Romans 5:1-11, he brings this foundational discussion about how we may be right with God to a close.

Of course, the foundation remains in place, in the same way that the pedestal of a statue always remains in place. But now a new topic is opened up: "God's love has been poured into our hearts[1] through the Holy Spirit", proclaims Paul triumphantly in verse 5. Paul begins to consider how we should live the Christian life, given that we now have **"peace with God"**, and the next major section of Romans up to the end of chapter 8 is dedicated to exploring and teaching exactly what a privilege and blessing this is, and what follows for living the Christian life.

### Peace with God

It's important to ask: What do we mean by "peace with God"? Today when people use this phrase it's often as a sense of peace, meaning a sense of tranquillity and wellbeing. When applied to God, this sense of tranquillity is often used to speak of a certainty or "peace" about a ▶

particular course of action, state of affairs, or decision that we are called upon to make.

But, as always, the best way to determine what the word means is to look at the way Paul uses the expression in this letter. As early as Romans 1:7, Paul has wished "grace and peace" upon the Roman Christians as gifts of "God our Father and the Lord Jesus Christ". This leads us to expect, especially given the link to the word "grace", that peace is not something achieved by us but given freely by God. This is re-affirmed by Romans 2:10, where "peace" is one of the things received by "everyone who does good". It's not a peace naturally shared by sinful humanity, as in Romans 3:17—"the way of peace they have not known".

And when, in Romans 5:10, Paul describes our prior state as having been "enemies", there can be no doubt that peace refers to a state rather than feelings; that is, the state of being at peace with God because of his grace and goodness, shown in Jesus Christ and his death on the cross. This may lead on to the tranquillity of feeling at peace with our God, but it is easy also to imagine situations (and Paul describes them in Romans 8) where tranquillity is the last thing we feel. Yet, if Jesus has died for our sins, we *are* at peace with God.

**Read Romans 5:1-11.**

**1.** What words or verses in Romans 5:1-11 describe our state, or who we were, before we trusted Jesus?

VERSE 8 SINNERS

ENEMIES OF GOD.

V - 10

**2.** Explain from the passage, and in your own words, how suffering can produce a good result.

**3.** The word "justified" (in verses 1 and 9) means "not guilty".

• When were we justified?

• What does this show about God's character?

**4.** What did Jesus do to bring about our justification? What earlier parts of Romans help us to answer this question?

**5.** What do we contribute to our justification?

**6.** Looking at the whole passage, what should be the immediate result, or results, of justification by faith?

**7.** What other, longer term results follow from our justification? In answering, explain what is meant by the term "much more" in 5:10.

**8.** *Group activity:* Break into pairs. One member of the pair plays the part of a non-Christian with a deep sense that they are not right with God. The other member of the pair explains how the person can be "not guilty", using Romans 5:1-9. Summarize your discussion in the group.

**9.** Looking at the idea of God's love in the passage:

- How is it the same as, or different from, human love?

- How do we know that God loves us?

- What result does God's love have in our lives?

# Rejoice in being boastful!

Do you remember the old children's song, "Joy is the flag flown high from the castle of my heart"? It's upbeat and boppy, and speaks of the way we rejoice when Jesus the King takes up residence in our lives. This word "rejoice" is used three times in most modern English translations of Romans 5 (verses 2, 3 and 11) and is therefore very important in thinking about how to apply the passage to our lives.

However, the Greek word translated as "rejoice" in this small section is translated everywhere else in Romans (and in the New Testament) not as "rejoicing" but as "boasting" or being "proud". So Jews "boast in the law" (2:23), and if Abraham had been justified by works he would have had "something to boast about, but not before God" (4:2).

If we carry this translation on into chapter 5, we "boast" in the hope of the glory of God (5:2), we "boast" in our sufferings (5:3) and we "boast" in God through our Lord Jesus Christ (5:11).

Now "rejoicing" certainly gets across some of the flavour of "boasting", because it's hard to imagine not rejoicing in something you were boasting about. But the emphasis is different. With boasting we are not so much focusing on the way we *feel*, but on the thing that we are boasting *about*. Now earlier in Romans Paul has strongly attacked one form of boasting; that is, a boasting centred upon human achievement or privilege (e.g. 2:23).

Here, however, Paul emphasizes that Christian "boasting" (and therefore joy and rejoicing) will happen on completely different grounds. Jews may boast in the racial privilege of being God's chosen people, with all that this implies. Greeks may boast of their wisdom in philosophy and eloquent speech. Others may boast for other reasons. Christians, however, will boast only because of what God has done for us in Jesus—or at least, that is what Paul insists ought to be the case, here in this passage.

In all this, we may well find cause for rejoicing. The point, however, is that we will never take pride in our achievement, but in Jesus' achievement on our behalf. He has justified us from sin, he will save us from God's wrath, and he has poured out God's love in our hearts through the Holy Spirit.

## » Implications

(Choose one or more of the following to think about further or to discuss in your group.)

- In what ways might our Christian lives be helped by using the word "boast" instead of "rejoice" in this passage?

- Compare Jeremiah 9:23-26. What are some of the things that humans are tempted to boast about:

  - according to Jeremiah?

  - according to Paul? (Note the parallel argument in 1 Corinthians 1:18-31.)

  - according to you?

- Using the passage, what do you think 'Christian boasting' would look like if you indulged in it in the coming week? In what situations could you do it?

- A Christian friend comes to you anxious that they are not right with God, despite having believed in Jesus' death for their sins. They are not aware of any specific serious wrongdoing in their lives. What could you say from Romans 5 to encourage them?

## » Give thanks and pray

- Thank God for the peace we have with God through the reconciliation of Jesus.
- Thank God for showing his love for us in sending Jesus not for the sake of the righteous, but for the sake of sinners.
- Pray that we would boast not in our own achievement, but in all that Jesus has done for us.

### Endnote

1. The 'heart', in the Bible, is neither a blood-pump nor a place where we feel emotion. The heart is really the 'centre of the human person', focusing particularly on that person's will and decision-making capacity, without neglecting the whole individual.

# THE FREE GIFT

## [ROMANS 5:12-21]

**1.** Do you think that there is an age at which children become sinful?

## Is your sin original?

IN ROMANS 5, PAUL OPERATES with two assumptions: first, that we are part of the **family** of Adam; and second, that we share the family likeness. By nature we are spiritually stillborn, and the choices we make reflect this internal deadness.

This is not automatically obvious to us. We tend to mythologize children as innocent, and it's true that because

**Extended family**

One of the reasons Western-minded Christians struggle with a passage like Romans 5:12-21 is that we tend to look at the individual and forget the whole. A man or ▶

woman is part of a family, and that family is part of an extended family, which in turn is part of a community or nation, which is part of humanity. We emphasize individual freedom and choice, and forget how greatly we are tied up with and affected by those around us, especially our families. Occasionally it will occur to us again that we are a part of the whole—for example, we will feel proud of our country's achievements in a way that simply doesn't make sense if we are nothing more than disconnected individuals.

of their helplessness and up to a certain age, babies are literally incapable of performing acts of sin. Sin, however, is not simply about doing bad things, but actually being bad to the bone; rotten to the core of our being, desiring to worship and serve created things rather than the Creator.

This predisposition, much as we like to deny it, is demonstrated for the world to see almost as soon as we become conscious and start to make choices for ourselves. More importantly, God knows both our actions and our heart. He sees the selfish and sinful nature from which our behaviour springs.

It may seem odd—or even harsh—that the choices of our ancestor(s) can affect us so markedly. But we rarely have difficulties with this in other areas of our lives; we simply accept that choices made by parents and grandparents about where to live, or where to go to school, have a huge impact on our lives. Especially when the choices have worked to our benefit—inheriting wealth, inheriting status—it is unlikely that we will complain. Neither then should we complain that to some extent, and even to a great extent, sin is part of our inheritance. Sin, born in us and confirmed by our choices, is something that we must take as a given.

Paul certainly takes it as a given. In fact, it's the first point in the dramatic contrast he draws between the 'givenness' of our sin in Adam, and the free gift of righteousness in Christ.

**Read Romans 5:1–11.**

**2.** How did sin come into the world?

**Read Romans 5:12-14.**

3. Explain the connection between sin, law and death in verses 12-14.

- How does sin lead to death?

- What is the role of the law? (Note how verse 14 helps in working out what 'law' means in verse 13.)

4. What does Paul mean when he speaks of "death"? Does he mean more than physical death, and if so, what? (You might like to compare Genesis 2:17, 3:19-24; and Romans 2:5, 8; 4:17.)

# The core of sin

Sin, its causes (as far as we can understand them) and its effects are drawn together with devastating clarity in this section of Paul's letter. When we look at the way Paul has described **sin** in the last five chapters, we begin to get some idea of the dimensions of this black stain on humanity.

It's important, if unappealing, to grasp this overall picture of sin, its root and its branches, because it is so easily underestimated by the ones who are subject to it. The view that Paul puts before us is of something that goes right to our very core, a moral blackness that can never be completely expunged without an extraordinary miracle of grace. As we contemplate this reality and come to understand how trapped we are by our own natures, the grandeur and majesty and sheer goodness of what God has done for us in Christ becomes ever more astonishing and worthy of praise.

## The vocabulary of sin

Here is a list of just some of the words Paul has used to describe sin in Romans to this point: ungodliness, futility in thinking, unrighteousness, foolish hearts darkened, impurity, error, lawbreaking, faithlessness, lawlessness, transgression, trespass, weakness, warfare ("enemies of God"), disobedience.

**Read Romans 5:12–21.**

5. What is "the free gift" (v. 15)?

6. Go through Romans 5:12-21 and fill in this table:

| Effects of sin | Effects of free gift |
| --- | --- |
|  |  |
|  |  |

**7.** Why is Christ's accomplishment so much greater than Adam's?

---

## » Implications

(Choose one or more of the following to think about further or to discuss in your group.)

- How has this passage, and the rest of Romans 1-5, helped you understand your sinfulness—its causes, its nature, its consequences? Summarize what you've learned.

- Back in Romans 1:16-17, Paul introduced his gospel as being powerful to save because it revealed "the righteousness of God". From Romans 5:12-21, and the rest of Romans 1-5, summarize in your own words what this means.

- How does Romans 5:12-21 help answer the person who asks, "What happens to those who have never heard the gospel?"

- By reviewing Romans up to this point, how can we find confidence and assurance that we are in Christ and no longer in Adam?

## » Give thanks and pray

- Thank God for the abundance of grace and the free gift of righteousness that reign in life through Jesus Christ.
- Pray that God would continue to reveal the sin in our lives, so that we might continue to become more obedient to him.
- What else does this passage, and the rest of Romans 1-5, prompt you to give thanks and pray for?

# ETERNAL LIFE BY GOOD DEEDS?

## [ROMANS 2:1-16]

THIS PASSAGE HAS BEEN MUCH debated over the centuries, and it is worth consulting the commentaries of CEB Cranfield and DJ Moo for more detail, but here are some brief comments that may be helpful.

Some of the verses in Romans 2—such as 6-7, 10 and 13-15—seem to leave open the possibility that someone might do enough good to win salvation. How can this be, especially in light of what Paul seems to be saying in the rest of his argument?

First of all, we must be careful not to interpret one part of Scripture so that it contradicts another, especially when the apparent contradiction is not just between books but between chapters written by the same author. Even ignoring the fact that God has spoken his word, we must regard it as highly unlikely that

Paul was so lazy and inattentive in what he wrote that he accidentally contradicted himself at a key point of his argument.

At the very least, then, we must notice that in Romans 1:19 Paul has insisted that although men and women know the plain truth about God, they've wilfully rejected and buried all knowledge of him. If this were not the case, then God wouldn't have any basis for judging and condemning those who fail to serve him.

What then are we to make of those who "by patience in well-doing seek for glory, honour and immortality" in Romans 2:7?

We ought to notice firstly that the key subject of this chapter, and indeed the entire section from 1:18-3:20, is not man but God. Paul is establishing here, and elsewhere in Romans, a key point about the nature of God: that God is completely fair and just. This requires, therefore, that God rewards those who do good. If he failed to do this according to his revealed standard, then there would be a dreadful failure of God's justice. This is so *whether or not* there is actually anyone who meets God's standard.

So then, is there such a person? If these verses were taken in isolation, we might well imagine that it is being implied that there *are* people who are good enough to warrant the reward of eternal life: Jews, perhaps, who follow the law to an acceptable standard, or Gentiles who do the best they can in accordance with their consciences. This is especially so if we notice that eternal life remains a gift and not a wage due (according to 2:7); that those who seek good in the same verse may simply be heading in the right direction rather than achieving perfection; and that the claim of a conscience which excuses (2:15) is, again, not the same as a claim to perfection. We may add to this the observation that God's law in the Old Testament *assumed* that people would sin and provided the means of forgiveness; so once again, perfect behaviour is not assumed.

As appealing as these possibilities are (and noting too that they don't ultimately exclude the possibility that we are still saved *only by faith* in Christ's death), they run counter to the context. There has been no hint in the beginning of this major section (1:18-32) that sin is anything but universal in scope—and that in its universality, the condemnation of humanity is perfectly justified. Nor, when we look to the end of the same major section (3:9-20), is there even the slightest hint that the law of God provides the faintest glimmer of hope for human performance. And as Paul sums up in 3:19-20, in words that recall and reinforce the ideas of 1:18, the whole point of his argument has been to show how fruitless the possibilities for righteousness are when we proceed under our own steam.

One final possibility is that the ones who receive the gift of eternal life and are justified are none other than Christians. Theologically speaking, this is perfectly true. It would however be unusual for Paul to jump ahead in his argument at this point to refer to Christians, when he has not yet spelt out how the death of Jesus brings Christians into being.

On the whole, then, it is wisest to understand the apparent references to people doing good, persisting in well-doing and excused by conscience to be an empty category that reflects on God's justice rather than our goodness. But if we opt for another alternative, we should understand that even so, Paul will go on to teach that being right with God can *only* happen through trust in the death of Jesus.

**Feedback on this resource** We really appreciate getting feedback about our resources—not just suggestions for how to improve them, but also positive feedback and ways they can be used. We especially love to hear that the resources may have helped someone in their Christian growth.

You can send feedback to us via the 'Feedback' menu in our online store, or write to us at PO Box 225, Kingsford NSW 2032, Australia.

# matthiasmedia

Matthias Media is an evangelical publishing ministry that seeks to persuade all Christians of the Bible-shaped, theological truth of God's purposes in Jesus Christ, and equip them with high-quality resources, so that they will:

- abandon their lives to the honour and service of Christ in daily holiness and decision-making
- pray constantly in Christ's name for the growth of his gospel
- speak the Bible's life-changing word whenever and however they can— in the home, in the world and in the fellowship of his people.

It was in 1988 that we first started pursuing this mission, and in God's kindness we now have more than 300 different ministry resources being used all over the world. These resources range from Bible studies and books through to training courses and audio sermons.

To find out more about our large range of very useful resources, and to access samples and free downloads, visit our website:

## www.matthiasmedia.com.au

---

## How to buy our resources

1. Direct from us over the internet:
   - in the US: www.matthiasmedia.com
   - in Australia and the rest of the world: www.matthiasmedia.com.au

2. Direct from us by phone:
   - in the US: 1 866 407 4530
   - in Australia: 1800 814 360
     (Sydney: 9663 1478)
   - international: +61-2-9663-1478

> Register at our website for our **free** regular email update to receive information about the latest new resources, **exclusive special offers**, and free articles to help you grow in your Christian life and ministry.

3. Through a range of outlets in various parts of the world. Visit **www.matthiasmedia.com.au/international.php** for details about recommended retailers in your part of the world, including www.thegoodbook.co.uk in the United Kingdom.

4. Trade enquiries can be addressed to:
   - in the US and Canada: sales@matthiasmedia.com
   - in Australia and the rest of the world: sales@matthiasmedia.com.au

# Other Interactive and Topical Bible Studies from Matthias Medi

Our Interactive Bible Studies (IBS) and Topical Bible Studies (TBS) are a valuable resource to help you keep feedin from God's word. The IBS series works through passages and books of the Bible; the TBS series pulls together th Bible's teaching on topics such as money or prayer. As at February 2010, the series contains the following titles:

## Beyond Eden
GENESIS 1-11
Authors: Phillip Jensen and
Tony Payne, 9 studies

## Out of Darkness
EXODUS 1-18
Author: Andrew Reid, 8 studies

## The Shadow of Glory
EXODUS 19-40
Author: Andrew Reid, 7 studies

## The One and Only
DEUTERONOMY
Author: Bryson Smith, 8 studies

## The Good, the Bad and the Ugly
JUDGES
Author: Mark Baddeley, 10 studies

## Famine and Fortune
RUTH
Authors: Barry Webb and
David Höhne, 4 studies

## Renovator's Dream
NEHEMIAH
Authors: Phil Campbell and
Greg Clarke, 7 studies

## The Eye of the Storm
JOB
Author: Bryson Smith, 6 studies

## The Search for Meaning
ECCLESIASTES
Author: Tim McMahon, 9 studies

## Two Cities
ISAIAH
Authors: Andrew Reid and
Karen Morris, 9 studies

## Kingdom of Dreams
DANIEL
Authors: Andrew Reid and
Karen Morris, 9 studies

## Burning Desire
OBADIAH AND MALACHI
Authors: Phillip Jensen and
Richard Pulley, 6 studies

## Warning Signs
JONAH
Author: Andrew Reid, 6 studies

## On That Day
ZECHARIAH
Author: Tim McMahon, 8 studies

## Full of Promise
THE BIG PICTURE OF THE O.T.
Authors: Phil Campbell
and Bryson Smith, 8 studies

## The Good Living Guide
MATTHEW 5:1-12
Authors: Phillip Jensen and
Tony Payne, 9 studies

## News of the Hour
MARK
Authors: Peter Bolt and Tony Payne,
10 studies

## Proclaiming the Risen Lord
LUKE 24-ACTS 2
Author: Peter Bolt, 6 studies

## Mission Unstoppable
ACTS
Author: Bryson Smith, 10 studies

## The Free Gift of Life
ROMANS 1-5
Author: Gordon Cheng, 8 studies

## The Free Gift of Sonship
ROMANS 6-11
Author: Gordon Cheng, 8 studies

## The Freedom of Christian Living
ROMANS 12-16
Author: Gordon Cheng, 7 studies

## Free for All
GALATIANS
Authors: Phillip Jensen
and Kel Richards, 8 studies

## Walk this Way
EPHESIANS
Author: Bryson Smith, 8 studies

## Partners for Life
PHILIPPIANS
Author: Tim Thorburn, 8 studies

## The Complete Christian
COLOSSIANS
Authors: Phillip Jensen and
Tony Payne, 8 studies

## To the Householder
1 TIMOTHY
Authors: Phillip Jensen and
Greg Clarke, 9 studies

## Run the Race
2 TIMOTHY
Author: Bryson Smith, 6 studies

## The Path to Godliness
TITUS
Authors: Phillip Jensen and
Tony Payne, 7 studies

## From Shadow to Reality
HEBREWS
Author: Joshua Ng, 10 studies

## The Implanted Word
JAMES
Authors: Phillip Jensen and
Kirsten Birkett, 8 studies

## Homeward Bound
1 PETER
Authors: Phillip Jensen and
Tony Payne, 10 studies

## All You Need to Know
2 PETER
Author: Bryson Smith, 6 studies

## The Vision Statement
REVELATION
Author: Greg Clarke, 9 studies

## Bold I Approach
PRAYER
Author: Tony Payne, 6 studies

## Cash Values
MONEY
Author: Tony Payne, 5 studies

## Sing for Joy
SINGING IN CHURCH
Author: Nathan Lovell, 6 studies

## The Blueprint
DOCTRINE
Authors: Phillip Jensen and
Tony Payne, 9 studies

## Woman of God
THE BIBLE ON WOMEN
Author: Terry Blowes, 8 studies